Sammy Sosa

By Jeff Savage

AMAZING ATHLETES

LERNER**SPORTS**/Minneapolis

Copyright © 2005 by Jeff Savage

This book is available in two editions:
Library binding by LernerSports
Soft cover by First Avenue Editions
Imprints of Lerner Publishing Group
241 First Avenue North
Minneapolis, MN 55401 U.S.A.

Website address: www.lernerbooks.com

Library of Congress Cataloging-in-Publication Data

Savage, Jeff, 1961–
       Sammy Sosa / by Jeff Savage.
           p.   cm. — (Amazing athletes)
       Summary: A biography of the Chicago Cubs outfielder known for his home run hitting and for doing humanitarian work in his native country, the Dominican Republic.
       Includes index.
       ISBN: 0–8225–3672–2 (lib. bdg. : alk. paper)
       ISBN: 0–8225–2041–9 (pbk. : alk. paper)
       1. Sosa, Sammy, 1968–Juvenile literature. 2. Baseball players—Dominican Republic Biography—Juvenile literature. [1. Sosa, Sammy, 1968– 2. Baseball players.] I. Savage, Jeff, 1961– Sammy Sosa, home run hero. II. Title. III. Series.
       GV865.S59S69 2005
       796.357'092—dc22   2003020147

Manufactured in the United States of America
1 2 3 4 5 6 – DP – 10 09 08 07 06 05

Table of Contents

Sammy Sosa sends a ball flying a long way.

SLAMMIN' SAMMY

Sammy Sosa swung his bat as hard as he could. *Crack!* The baseball soared through the air like a rocket. Sammy hopped sideways over home plate, like he always does when he knows he's hit a **home run.** The ball sailed far over the right field wall, a whopping 490 feet away.

Sammy's Chicago Cubs were playing the Colorado Rockies in this 2002 game at Colorado's Coors Field. Sammy's three-run homer gave his Cubs a 4–0 lead in the third inning. But Sammy wasn't finished yet. In the next inning, he came up to bat again. Rockies pitcher Shawn Chacon fired a pitch over the plate. Sammy swung hard. *Boom!* The ball flew over the center field fence for another home run.

Sammy hops over home plate as he watches a ball fly over the fence.

Sammy pumps his fist as he rounds the bases.

Sammy circled the bases with a smile. He stepped on home plate and gave his usual thump-kiss salute. He thumped his chest with his fist and then kissed his fingers twice. The first kiss was for his mother. The second kiss was for his friends and fans.

In the fifth inning, Sammy stepped into the **batter's box** again. The fans rose to their feet. Rockies pitcher Mark Corey threw a fastball down the middle. Sammy swung. *Bam!* The ball whistled over the left field wall. Another home run!

Sammy makes a big swing at another pitch.

Sammy points to the sky after touching home plate.

After his third trip around the bases, Sammy got high fives from his teammates in the Cubs dugout. *"Sam-mee! Sam-mee!"* the fans yelled. Sammy stepped from the dugout and waved. "What a great feeling," Sammy said afterward. "I am glad that they appreciate me." Thanks to Sammy, the Cubs won the game, 15–1.

Baseball is the most popular sport in Sammy's home country, the Dominican Republic.

LEARNING THE GAME

Samuel Peralta Sosa was born November 12, 1968, to Juan and Lucrecya Sosa. Sammy grew up in the Dominican Republic, a small Caribbean island nation about six hundred miles from Florida.

Like Sammy's father, many Dominicans work in the sugarcane fields. It is hard work.

Most Dominicans are poor. Sammy's family lived in a town called San Pedro de Macoris. Their home was a two-room unit of an old hospital. Sammy shared his room with his four brothers and two sisters. They slept on foam pads on the floor.

Sammy's father worked in the sugarcane fields. His mother sold food on the streets. Together, they barely made enough money to feed their children.

Sammy was seven years old when his father died. Sammy and his brothers and sisters had to take jobs to help the family survive. Sammy shined shoes and sold fruit on the street. He had to quit school in the eighth grade to work. He washed cars during the day and worked as a janitor at night.

Many great baseball players have come from the Dominican Republic. Manny Ramirez of the Boston Red Sox, Vladimir Guerrero of the Anaheim Angels, Miguel Tejada of the Baltimore Orioles, and Rafael Furcal of the Atlanta Braves all were born in Sammy's home country.

Baseball is a popular sport in the Dominican Republic. Children play the game on dirt fields with beat-up bats and worn balls. Sometimes kids even play with broomsticks and oranges.

Sammy did not start playing baseball until he was 13 years old. He was skinny, but he swung the bat very hard. Sammy saw other Dominican baseball players become stars in the United States. "They lived in beautiful houses," said Sammy. "It would be nice to live like that."

Sammy began taking baseball lessons. The lessons cost 67 cents a week. Sammy's brothers worked extra to help pay for the lessons. Sammy practiced at a dirt field near his home. Sometimes he practiced all day long. Sammy never wanted to quit. "Más [more]!" he would yell. Sammy was determined to work hard and become great.

Sammy got his start in Major League Baseball with the Texas Rangers.

GOING PLACES

Sammy joined a local **Little League** team. Before long, a **scout** for a Major League Baseball team spotted him. The scout was impressed with Sammy's skills. The Texas Rangers offered Sammy a **contract** to play for one of its **minor league** teams. Sammy was 16 years old.

The Rangers paid Sammy $3,500 to sign the contract. Sammy felt rich! He proudly gave the money to his mother. He kept just a few dollars for himself to buy his first bicycle.

Early in 1986, Sammy hugged his family goodbye. He flew on an airplane to the United States to join a Rangers' minor league team in Florida. That year, he had a **batting average** of .275 and hit 19 **doubles.** A year later, he improved to 11 homers and 27 doubles. Scouts called him a top **prospect.** They believed he was a future star.

In 1989, the Rangers brought him up to the major leagues. "It was the happiest day of my life," Sammy said. In his first major league game, Sammy played right field against the New York Yankees. He rapped a **single** for his first **big league** hit. Five nights later, he hit a home run off ace pitcher Roger Clemens.

In some games, Sammy hit home runs and made good plays in the field. But other times, Sammy struck out a lot and had a hard time getting hits.

Most baseball players spend their whole careers in the minor leagues. Only the very best become Major League Baseball players.

The White Sox believed Sammy could be a superstar player.

Other teams started to notice Sammy. That same year, the Chicago White Sox traded for him. Sammy moved to Chicago and became a member of the White Sox.

The Sox paid Sammy $500,000 for the season. He bought a house for his mother, a hair salon for his sisters, and fancy cars for his brothers. Sammy played well for the White Sox in 1990. He hit 15 home runs, 26 doubles, and 10 **triples.** He even had 32 stolen bases. Following the 1991 season, the Chicago Cubs traded for Sammy.

Sammy became an instant fan favorite with the White Sox.

Sammy battled injuries his first year with the Cubs.

SWINGING FOR THE FENCES

Sammy struggled with injuries during his first season with the Cubs. He played in only 67 games.

That **off-season** Sammy worked hard to get in great shape. In 1993, he returned to the field even stronger than before. Sammy became a home run-hitting machine. He hit 33 home runs that year, 25 the next, then 36, then 40. He was even selected to play in the 1995 **All-Star Game.**

Sammy had become a hero in Chicago and throughout the United States. In the Dominican Republic, children dreamed of being like Sammy. "Sammy has given so much hope to so many people, especially those in poor countries," said Omar Minaya, "He has shown that with hard work you can make it."

Cubs fans soon realized they had a special player in Sammy Sosa.

In 1998, Sammy and Mark McGwire of the Saint Louis Cardinals thrilled baseball fans with their home run heroics.

In 1997, the Cubs rewarded Sammy with a four-year contract for $42 million. He paid his team back a year later with a monster season. Throughout the summer of 1998, Sammy and Saint Louis Cardinals first baseman Mark McGwire smacked home runs at an incredible pace.

The record for most home runs in a season was 61. By early September, Sammy and McGwire were both about to break the record. McGwire did it first, belting home run number 62 against Sammy's Cubs. Sammy raced in from right field to congratulate McGwire.

Sammy congratulates Mark McGwire after McGwire breaks the single-season home run record.

50 SAN DIEGO
40 ARIZONA

25 MC GWIRE   70
21 SOSA   66

Sammy and Mark McGwire's run for the record has come to be known as the Great Home Run Race.

Five days later at the Cubs' Wrigley Field, Sammy joined the fun. He hit two home runs against the Milwaukee Brewers to break the record too. McGwire ended the season with 70 home runs. Sammy finished with 66, and he also led the majors in **runs batted in (RBI),** with 158.

In 1998, a terrible hurricane hit Sammy's home country. Thousands of homes were destroyed.

HOME RUN HERO

Sammy and the Cubs reached the 1998 **playoffs** but lost to the Atlanta Braves. Sammy was disappointed, but he had other worries. A hurricane had struck the Dominican Republic. Thousands of people were homeless. Sammy and his wife, Sonia, flew home to help. Sammy passed out food to people in need. He raised millions of dollars to help rebuild the country.

Dominicans held a parade for Sammy and his wife, Sonia, when they returned home after the Great Home Run Race.

In 1999, Sammy bashed 63 homers to lead all baseball players that year. He hit 50 homers in 2000, then smacked 64 more in 2001 to become the first player in baseball history to hit 60 or more homers in three seasons. In 2002, he clubbed 49. He finished one home run short of becoming the first player to hit 50 or more homers five years in a row.

In April 2003, Sammy hit his 500th home run. He was the 18th player to hit that many home runs in his career. He smacked a total of 40 that season and led the Cubs to the playoffs. Sammy and his team came within a few outs of reaching the **World Series.** Even though they ended up losing to the Florida Marlins, Sammy and the Cubs had had an incredible season.

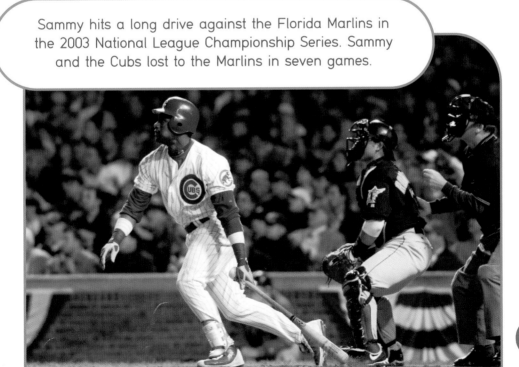

Sammy hits a long drive against the Florida Marlins in the 2003 National League Championship Series. Sammy and the Cubs lost to the Marlins in seven games.

With star pitchers Greg Maddux *(left)*, Kerry Wood *(center)*, and Mark Prior, the Cubs were ready for a big season in 2004.

In 2004, Sammy was the biggest star on a team of great players. Sammy's teammates included Greg Maddux, Kerry Wood, Mark Prior, Nomar Garciaparra, Moises Alou, and Corey Patterson.

Everyone expected the Cubs to make the playoffs. Many people thought the Cubs would win the World Series. But Sammy hurt his back early in the season. He missed several games. When he returned, he struggled. Sammy hit just 35 home runs with a batting average of .253. Several Cubs players also missed games because of injuries.

Sammy and his teammates played hard. But they failed to reach the playoffs. It was a disappointing season, and Sammy plans to do better in 2005.

Sammy and his son, Sammy Jr., spend a few minutes on the field together. Sammy enjoys spending time with his family.

Sammy is a fan favorite among children and adults alike. They love how he plays hard and is always smiling for his fans. "When I was young," he says, "I was dreaming that I would be here in America. Now that I am here, every day is like a holiday for me. Every time I wake up, I say, 'God Bless America.'"

Sammy is grateful to all the baseball fans who have supported him over the years.

Selected Career Highlights

2004   Played in his seventh All-Star Game

2003   Became the eighteenth Major League Baseball player to hit 500 home runs in his career
Achieved his 2,000 career hit
Helped lead the Cubs to the playoffs and the National League Championship Series

2002   Won the National League home run title, with 49
Scored the fourth-most runs in the majors for the season, with 122
Played in his sixth All-Star Game

2001   Led the majors in runs batted in for the season, with 160
Finished with 64 home runs, the second-most in baseball that season
Led the major leagues in runs scored that season, with 146
Played in his fifth All-Star Game

2000   Won the Major League Baseball home run title, with 50
Finished second in the National League in runs batted in, with 138
Played in his fourth All-Star Game

1999   Hit 63 home runs
Finished third in the league in runs batted in, with 141
Played in his third All-Star Game

1998   Hit 66 home runs, the third-most homers in a single season in Major League Baseball history
Led the majors in runs batted in, with 158
Led the majors in runs scored, with 134
Named National League Most Valuable Player
Played in his second All-Star Game
Received Roberto Clemente Award for community service

Glossary

All-Star Game: a game played every July in which the best players from each of the major leagues face off

batter's box: the area next to home plate where the batter stands

batting average: a number that describes how often a baseball player makes a base hit

big league: a nickname for one of the two top groups of North American professional baseball teams. One group is the National League, and the other is the American League. They are also called the major leagues.

contract: a written agreement between a player and a team

doubles: hits that let the batter safely reach second base

home run: a hit that lets the batter circle the bases safely to cross home plate and score a run. They are sometimes called homers.

Little League: a popular organization that sponsors baseball for boys and girls

minor league: one of a number of groups of teams throughout the United States and Canada where players improve their playing skills. Many minor league teams are owned by major league teams.

off-season: the time between seasons when many players train and practice to improve and stay in shape

playoffs: a series of games played after a regular season to determine which teams will play in a championship

prospect: a player whom scouts believe will be a good major league player

runs batted in (RBIs): the number of runners able to score on a batter's action, such as a hit or a walk

scout: in baseball, a person who judges the skills of players

single: a hit that lets the batter safely reach first base

triples: hits that let the batter safely reach third base

World Series: baseball's championship. In Major League Baseball, the National League and American League each hold a championship series at the end of the regular season. The winning teams from each league meet each other in the World Series.

Further Reading & Websites

Christopher, Matt. *At the Plate with Sammy Sosa.* Boston: Little Brown & Company, 1999.

Driscoll, Laura. *Sammy Sosa: He's the Man.* New York: Grosset & Dunlap, 1999.

Savage, Jeff. *Sammy Sosa: Home Run Hero.* Minneapolis: LernerSports, 2000.

Torres, John Albert. *Sports Great Sammy Sosa.* Berkeley Heights, NJ: Enslow Publishers, 2003.

Chicago Cubs: The Official Site
http://www.chicagocubs.com
The official website of the Chicago Cubs features the latest team news, as well as Cubs history, statistics, and much more. The Players section includes Sammy Sosa's biography, statistics, and career highlights.

Latino Sports Legends Website
http://www.latinosportslegends.com
This website features many great Latino sports figures, including Sammy Sosa.

The Official Site of Major League Baseball
http://www.mlb.com
Major League Baseball's website has all the latest scores and game schedules, as well as information on players, teams, and baseball history.

Sports Illustrated for Kids
http:www.sikids.com
The *Sports Illustrated for Kids* website covers all sports, including baseball.

Index

Photo Acknowledgments

Photographs are used with the permission of: © Reuters/CORBIS, pp. 4, 7, 8, 27; © Ray Stubblebine/Icon SMI, p. 5; © AP/Wide World Photos, pp. 6, 9, 14, 21, 22, 23, 24; © Tony Arruza/CORBIS, p. 10; © Getty Images, pp. 13, 16, 17, 18, 20; © John McDonough/Icon SMI, p. 19; © John Gress/Icon SMI, p. 25; © Jeff Topping/Reuters/CORBIS, p. 26; © Albert Dickson/Sporting News/Icon SMI, p. 28; © Gary Rothstein/Icon SMI, p. 29.

Front Cover: © MLB Photos via Getty Images.